Rugby Rivals

Published by Accent Press Ltd – 2011

ISBN 9781907726644

The Quick Reads project in Wales is a joint venture between the Welsh
Assembly Government and the Welsh Books Council. Titles are
funded as part of the National Basic Skills Strategy for Wales.

Printed and bound in the UK

Cover design by Adam Walker

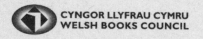

CYNGOR LLYFRAU CYMRU
WELSH BOOKS COUNCIL

Noddir gan
Lywodraeth Cynulliad Cymru
Sponsored by
Welsh Assembly Government

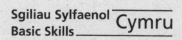

Sgiliau Sylfaenol
Basic Skills ——— Cymru

Rugby Rivals

My Top Ten Players

Martyn Williams

ACCENT PRESS LTD

Introduction

During my career, I've been privileged to play against and alongside some of the greatest rugby players of all time. Choosing my top ten for this book has been a really difficult task, but also an enjoyable one as it's brought back some very happy memories.

When I look at the players I've picked, I see they all have a couple of things in common. First, they are hard men, tough as nails, every one of them. Second, they also all have an attitude that I admire.

To be a really top player, you've got to have a competitive edge and mental strength. And for me, a great player has longevity, the ability to stay at the top for a long, long time and sustain his standards.

I've seen lots of players come in, have one or two good years, then think they've made it, drop their standards and fade away as a result.

But when you start to make it, that's when you've got to start working harder again. Everybody has dips in form. That's just the way it is. It's natural. Nobody can play at the very top of their game throughout their career, apart from maybe Richie McCaw!

But what all ten of these players have shown is consistency. They've stayed at the top for so long because they haven't let their standards slip and they've kept on working at their game.

They've also all got that mental toughness. Everybody stresses how very physical the game is these days and how everybody is quicker, bigger and stronger than they used to be – and they are, no doubt about that. But what stands out more than anything about these ten is how mentally strong they are. At the top level, rugby is as much a mental game as a physical one.

We've all trained with athletes who are fantastic when it comes to fitness testing in training and the weights they can lift. But when it comes to the game, they don't deliver.

The ten players I've selected – in no particular order – have all shown they can do it when it matters.

And they are all hugely competitive in anything they do. Whether it's touch rugby or tiddlywinks, they want to win.

So it's all about attitude and desire.

The bottom line is that rugby hurts, all the

more so at the top level. You've got to want to do it. You can't cruise through it. You've got to give your all and that's what these players have done throughout their careers.

I consider myself hugely fortunate to have shared a rugby field with all of them.

Chapter One

MARTIN JOHNSON

To my mind, the truly great players aren't just the ones who can do the job out on the pitch. They are also people who have an influence on others off the field, and Martin Johnson certainly falls into that category.

Johnno did everything in the game, including the ultimate honour of leading England to World Cup glory in 2003, and of course he's gone on to lead his country as team manager since hanging up his boots.

He's probably the greatest captain of the professional era, having also skippered the British and Irish Lions on two tours.

I was lucky enough to go on the second of those trips – to Australia in 2001 – and to play under him.

Up until then, I'd only ever played against him and been on the end of few hammerings from his England team.

Because of their size, you think people like him are larger-than-life, intimidating figures.

And that image was reinforced for me after watching the behind-the-scenes *Living with Lions* video of the 1997 tour of South Africa, when he led the Lions to a memorable series win. He was such an imposing presence on that video. I always remember the scene when he was having a nasty eye injury stitched up in the dressing room, and he just couldn't wait to get back out on the pitch.

So it was a daunting prospect to be a team-mate of this massive figure.

But when I got to know him in the Lions team on the 2001 trip Down Under, I found he was a down-to-earth bloke and he really made me feel at ease.

We both love American Football, so that was an interest we had in common, and I really enjoyed his company.

But when it came to the business of rugby, he was very focused. What stood out for me on that 2001 tour were the standards he set, day-in, day-out, in training.

The English players who had known him for a while said his training sessions were always like that.

If he was carrying a bump he would still be out there. He would never sit back and think: *I'm the England captain and I can rest on my laurels.*

He always set an example. And he would never ask people to do something he wasn't prepared to do himself. He backed his words with his actions and led by example. No one wanted to let him down. You couldn't have anything but total respect for the bloke.

He is very knowledgeable about the game of rugby as well. You have this picture of second row forwards as being dour, hard-nosed, heads-down characters, but Johnno's a very intelligent man.

He knows what he wants, he's very focused and he knows the game inside out.

Even back then, he would talk about players in Wales, and surprise you by knowing who they were.

He was also very modest. One of his favourite sayings was: "A great team makes a great captain, but a great captain can't make a great team."

A lot of people have asked me what he was like in the dressing room, because I think they expect him to have come out with Churchillian speeches before games.

I expected that myself, to be honest. But he didn't actually say much on that 2001 tour. We did have big characters out there, like Keith

Wood, the Irish hooker who was an emotional guy and would do a lot of talking.

But, although Johnno didn't say much, when he did speak, you knew it would be important. People would sit back and take note.

He would be short, but to the point.

He didn't show his emotions as much as others might, but he was very precise and forceful. Some captains say too little, some too much. He got the balance just right. I think that's an art

When you think of the characters and size of personalities he had to captain during his career – people like Wood, Lawrence Dallaglio, Austin Healey, Matt Dawson – you can imagine the skill needed to control them. But he was always the dominant figure.

Some players just have that presence and he was one of them.

He certainly had a presence out on the field itself. I think he was one of the hardest players I've ever played against.

For me, hardness isn't about stamping on somebody on the floor. That's not hard. Hard, to me, is somebody who, week-in, week-out, puts his body on the line and takes as much as he gives. And Johnno did that throughout his career.

He was also exactly what you want out of your second row. You want a lock to be someone you hate playing against and he was certainly that.

He was an absolute pain to play against. He was such a big man and got in all the wrong places. He would climb all over you in the line-out and his size was a real nuisance in rucks and mauls.

He was the epitome of a hard, no-nonsense rugby player who was willing to put his body on the line and expected others to do the same.

I remember reading a quote from him once where he said the thing that really frustrated him was when players pulled out injured or because they were carrying niggles.

He said there was no way you could play rugby for a season without being injured or having niggles. That's part and parcel of the game. I think he has that touch of Leicester mentality which the Tigers built their success on, of which he was a big part.

But the guy wasn't just hard. He was also a talented rugby player. Technically he was a very good line-out forward, his angles of running and off-loading were good, and his work-rate was just huge.

He was always there making the tackles or the hard yards. That was shown by that little rumble he went on before Jonny Wilkinson dropped the winning drop-goal in the World Cup final against Australia.

Jonny took the glory, but the position wouldn't have been created if Johnno hadn't made those couple of yards. That was his mantra. You go forward, you go forward again and then you claim the points. And then you do it again.

So he had all the skills you need in a world-class second row, but he had that presence as well, and his record as a leader speaks for itself.

He's also got a bit of real class to him, as I found out last year.

When we were arranging the events for my testimonial, we decided it would be good to put something on to coincide with the England–Wales game, so we arranged a dinner for the Thursday night at Twickenham.

I thought it would be good to get the two coaches – Johnno and Warren Gatland – together for a question and answer session at the dinner.

It fell to me to ring him up. It was getting close to the event and I was nervous. I was thinking "I've got to ring Martin Johnson here."

The event was two nights before the Wales game and the England coach would have a lot on his plate at that time. But he agreed to do it. He came along and he was fantastic.

For me, that sums him up. He wasn't too busy to do something for a fellow rugby man, and I'll never forget that.

As I say, it's that class and presence both on and off the field that sets the greats apart from the run-of-the-mill players, and Johnno has that presence in spades.

Chapter Two

JONAH LOMU

As part of my job, I attend quite a few events aimed at getting young children interested in the game of rugby. You tend to find that quite a few kids don't know the names of current players. But they all seem to know the name of one player – Jonah Lomu.

And some of them weren't even born when Jonah was at the peak of his powers.

That's a tribute to the lasting legacy of the giant New Zealand winger – a man who brought the game of rugby to a whole new audience.

Although it's almost a decade since Lomu last played international rugby, the young kids know about him from their video games or the clips on YouTube.

Those clips will live on for ever, ensuring that he will remain a legend of the game for generations. There's never been anyone else quite like Jonah.

He couldn't have come along at a better time for the game of rugby, really, as his emergence coincided with the sport going professional in 1995. At a time when rugby needed to make an impact, he was the perfect person to come on the scene.

He did a huge amount for the sport in terms of raising its profile, and taking it to a wider audience.

He wasn't just a rugby superstar, but a sporting superstar, whose fame transcended the game.

Whether you liked rugby or not, you knew who Jonah Lomu was. Everybody had heard of him and that remains the case today.

Like everyone else, I watched in amazement as he burst on the scene at the 1995 World Cup in South Africa. I was nineteen at the time and just starting out with my home-town club of Pontypridd. I remember being stunned by what I was watching on TV. This bloke ran riot.

We'd never seen anything like it before, nobody had. He was as big as a second row and as quick as any back. He was an incredible athlete who took the game to a higher level.

Top-flight rugby is full of big men now. A lot of players are huge physically, including some threequarters. But back then it was unheard of to have a winger of that size.

Jonah was just unstoppable. He was so big and quick, but he also had good feet for such a big bloke and was very agile. Together those attributes set him apart from anybody else.

No one who saw it will ever forget what he did to England in the semi-final of the '95 World Cup in Cape Town, when he ran over the likes of Mike Catt and Tony Underwood as he helped himself to four tries. It was simply staggering. He was the difference between the sides.

More than fifteen years on, you still see footage of his exploits in that match on a pretty regular basis. That's just how amazing it was.

The impact he had on the sport was huge.

No one knew how to stop him and he sent fear into the ranks of any team that faced him.

So you can imagine how I felt a couple of years later when I found out I was going to be playing against him.

It was for Wales A against New Zealand at Pontypridd's Sardis Road in 1997.

He was the focus for the whole week in the build-up to the game. The question was: how are we going to stop Jonah Lomu? And I'm sure that was the question for every team that played against him back then.

It was a scary experience, to say the least. I missed him a couple of times, but I did manage to tackle him twice, which was a real badge of honour.

To be honest, it was very rare to see one-on-

one tackles on him back then. You would have to send in at least two or three boys on him, otherwise you wouldn't have a hope.

As great a team as New Zealand were, back then you weren't playing the All Blacks, you were playing Jonah Lomu. That's how much he dominated the sport during those years.

I also played against him in the full Wales team five years later in Cardiff in November 2002. That turned out to be his last game for New Zealand. He'd been through some very difficult times by then, having been diagnosed with a serious kidney complaint.

He was only twenty seven, but it was remarkable that he'd managed to keep playing Test rugby as long as he had, given the extent of his health problems.

The courage he showed battling against his illness added to the stature of the man. He went through a hell of lot, but always retained his dignity.

I was able to see those qualities at first hand when he joined the Cardiff Blues in the autumn of 2006.

I'd heard a rumour in pre-season that we might be signing him, but I'd just thought: *You've got to be joking.*

It wasn't a joke, though. He really was coming to Cardiff.

It was a great coup for the region and all anybody spoke about for weeks. It was huge for us to get him and the publicity we received was amazing.

That's the effect he still had on everybody, even though he'd been away from the international scene for some time and out of the game altogether for a while due to his illness.

I remember there was a big press conference at the Arms Park to announce his signing, where crowds of media turned up even though the big man himself wasn't here yet.

At that conference, the great Gareth Edwards – who is on the board at the Blues – said it was like Cardiff City signing Maradona. That summed it up.

There was an even bigger media circus surrounding Jonah's debut against the Italian club Calvisano and that circus stayed in town throughout his stay.

It was surreal to have him as a team-mate. You sometimes don't think famous people are real. But he was really down to earth. He was easy to get along with and had no airs and graces about him whatsoever. He just wanted to work hard and get back into rugby. You felt for him because he'd fought so hard to get over his illness, but then, just when he seemed to be getting back to his old self, he would pick up a little niggle.

In the end, he was only with us for a short while, his stay cut short by injury. But he was great for us in terms of the interest he created. He was still able to put bums on seats like no one else in the game.

He was also a great example to our young players, in terms of how professional and dedicated he was.

But, above all, he was just a really good bloke. He paid for a new sound system down at the Blues training base and he could have taken it with him, but he left it for the boys.

That summed him up. He was very generous and a real gentleman. If ever the phrase "Gentle Giant" was appropriate to use for someone, then it was with him.

It was a privilege to know him and it's something special to be able to say you've played with Jonah Lomu.

He's been great for the game of rugby and the way he fought against his illness has been an inspiration to people around the world.

There will only ever be one Jonah Lomu.

Chapter Three

SHANE WILLIAMS

Shane Williams was probably a victim of the Lomu legacy in the early years of his career. After Jonah, there was a feeling that all wingers needed to be huge. But Shane has proved that notion wrong in unforgettable style.

It can't have been easy for him starting out at the end of the 1990s. Everyone was looking to have big wingers. Wales had Gareth Thomas and Dafydd James, England had Ben Cohen and Dan Luger, Ireland had Shane Horgan, Australia had Joe Roff, New Zealand had Lomu and Tana Umaga ... and so on.

The common consensus was that wings had to be 6ft plus and at least 13 or 14 stone. And there was Shane, all of 5ft 7ins and about 11st wringing wet.

Nevertheless, he still made enough of an impression at club level to force his way into the Wales set-up for the 2000 Six Nations championship.

When he first came into the squad, he was a very quiet, unassuming little fast kid that they'd pulled up from Neath. Nobody knew much about him and he didn't say much.

But he did his talking on the pitch during that championship, scoring three tries against Scotland and Italy to provoke the first burst of Shane-mania.

His picture was all over the papers and he was hailed as the bright new star of Welsh rugby, his fancy footwork and fresh-faced enthusiasm immediately catching the public's imagination.

But, after that great start, he lost his place in the national team towards the end of 2001 and then drifted off the scene for a couple of years.

A lot of people probably thought he wouldn't come back, because everybody was still looking for bigger players. They seemed to be the way forward.

But then he proved them wrong, starting with one particular game at the 2003 World Cup.

Shane had just squeezed into the Wales squad on the back of being able to provide cover at scrum-half, which is the position he started out in at his home-town club of Amman United.

He was very much a fringe figure in the

squad and didn't play in the opening three group games.

He was then just chucked in for the final pool match against New Zealand in Sydney. The side was thrown together for that game, and given little hope. Indeed, Shane himself almost didn't make it as he was ill in bed the week before the game.

But he managed to recover in time and the rest is history. He announced himself on the world stage that night with a brilliant display for Wales, giving the All Blacks a huge fright.

It goes to show how fickle sport can be. If he hadn't played in that New Zealand game, he might never have played for Wales again.

Instead, he showed what he could do that night, and has never looked back.

He's gone on to be a vital player in two Grand Slams, was World Player of the Year in 2008, and Wales's all-time record try scorer. Not bad for a little fella.

I've no hesitation in saying that Shane is the most naturally gifted rugby player I've ever been on a field with. He is an absolute genius – and in my eyes he's got to be up there with the greats from the 1970s.

Some of the things he does in training are incredible. When you play touch rugby, it's not fair when he's on the other side. Some days he is basically unmarkable. I don't care who you are. You can be the best defender in the world, but if he's on his game there's nothing you can do.

I've played against him many times over the years and he's skinned me plenty of times. You know what he's going to do, but you can't stop him because he is so quick on his feet.

If he's got a little bit of space and is running at you at full pace, you haven't got a hope. He may not be a giant, but he's still a scary sight. It's deceptive – he's such a strong little bugger. You try to hit him around the chest, but he's got this amazing knack of wriggling out of tackles.

People have talked about his size throughout his career, but he rarely misses a tackle. He's a very good defender and he'll have guys twice his size trying to tackle him and will bounce off them. He's so gutsy and tough.

But he's also got great footballing skills and can do a very effective little chip and chase if the situation demands.

He's just good at anything when it comes to sport. You can see that when he plays football. He's a natural. People have tried to play on his height over the years by putting cross kicks on him, but he's so spring-heeled he is able to deal with that.

His ability to deal with high balls was once seen as a weakness because of his height, but he's worked really hard on the timing of his leap to counter that. With the height he gets in the air and how good he is at taking the ball, it's not a problem any more.

I remember one catch he took in the Six Nations game against Scotland in Cardiff last year when he seemed to be hanging in the air. It was incredible, and it really lifted the crowd and the whole Welsh team.

The reason why I've got so much admiration for him is that he's worked at every single aspect of his game to make sure he has no weaknesses. He knows what players have tried to target him on and he's made a big effort to work on those areas. In particular, he's worked on his upper body strength and bulked up.

All that work culminated in what he achieved in 2008 when he was named World Player of the Year.

I can't remember a Welsh player ever playing as well as he did during that year. He was untouchable.

Would we have won the Six Nations Grand Slam if Shane hadn't been playing that season? I doubt it very much.

He scored six tries during that championship

campaign and made a crucial difference out in Ireland and in the title-clincher against France. Both were really tight matches with little to choose between the sides and his brilliance just gave us the edge, when he came up with a couple of superb individual tries.

As well as scoring the only try of the match against Ireland in Dublin, he also showed his all-round ability by stepping in at scrum-half for ten minutes when Mike Phillips was in the sin-bin. He did a great job and I think he really enjoyed it. It showed what a natural rugby player he is and what great passing skills he has.

Then that summer he went down to South Africa with Wales and was absolutely superb. I watched those Tests from back home because I was injured.

The try he scored in the second Test in Pretoria was a real gem, as he sent about five Springboks the wrong way with a little shimmy. Very few players can do that kind of thing and you could just sit back and enjoy watching him weave his magic.

When you think what's he gone on to do, it's amazing he was out of the team for so long. Thank goodness for that New Zealand game in 2003.

Over the years I've had people question whether I am too small for my position, so I can really empathise with Shane and the efforts he's made to more than compensate for his smaller stature.

He's proof yet again that great rugby players can come in all shapes and sizes.

So what about Jonah and Shane as the perfect wing pairing? Little and Large and absolutely lethal!

Chapter Four

DAN CARTER

I had the privilege of being there at the very start of Dan Carter's international career – not that I felt particularly privileged at the time!

It was in Hamilton, back in June 2003, and I was captain of Wales for the Test match against New Zealand that ended our summer tour Down Under.

I felt we'd given a fair account of ourselves the week before in Sydney, when we were in the game against Australia for a good while before in the end losing 30–10.

But it was to be a different story against the All Blacks. We suffered a record 55–3 defeat and it was a painful day all round, with Colin Charvis being laid out in a collision with Jerry Collins, while I was left with an ugly facial wound that needed half a dozen stitches.

We were given a real lesson and, if truth be told, it was men against boys.

In theory, Kiwi Carter should have been one of the 'boys' in that contest, given that he was only twenty-one. But he showed a maturity way beyond his years as he marked his Test debut with a 20 point haul.

As far as I can remember, he hadn't been mentioned much in the build-up to the game.

Our coach at the time was a Kiwi, Steve Hansen, and he knew all the All Blacks inside out.

I remember him going through all their players in the days before the game, giving us the low-down on their strengths and weaknesses. But when it came to Carter, he'd just said, "Oh and they've got this new up-and-coming kid from Canterbury in the centre."

So we didn't know much about him going into the game. But we certainly did afterwards!

As he was playing at inside centre, he was up against Mark Taylor, who was an excellent defender and as strong as an ox. Mark had been on the international scene for the best part of a decade by then and was very experienced.

But Carter was totally unfazed. He was just class that day – outstanding, considering it was his first Test match – and he really announced himself on the international stage.

It wasn't long before he moved in field to take up the reins at outside-half and he's been a sensation there ever since.

There have been some great fly-halves in the world game during my career, people like Jonny Wilkinson, Matt Giteau, Neil Jenkins, Juan-Martin Hernandez, Stephen Jones and Ronan O'Gara. But I think Carter has been the best of the lot.

People may say he plays in a great side and that it's easy to play at 10 in that New Zealand team, but they are not the same team without him.

If you look at his game, he's got everything. His kicking is as good as anybody's, he's quick, he's elusive, he's got great feet, he's got great distribution skills, he's defensively strong and he runs the game as well.

A lot of 10s may have his skills or his speed, but perhaps haven't got his kicking game and are not as attackingly astute. With other fly-halves, it's the other way round. They've got the tactical ability, but not the flair.

With Carter, you've got the complete package. He kicks when he should kick, he runs when he should run and reads the game superbly. He's the complete player.

Outside-half has become a different kind of role during the course of my career.

Back in the days before professionalism, the

27

fly-half was seen as a little will-o'-the-wisp character jinking his way through the opposition. But with the game changing and players becoming so much bigger, that kind of 10 has been left behind. Fly-halves these days have to be able to hold their own physically and stand up in defence. So they tend to be far more robust characters.

What's so good about Carter is that he can cope with that physical side of the game, but he's also got the flair and pace that the little wizards like Barry John and Phil Bennett had in the 1970s. That's what makes him the perfect 10.

I've played against him quite a few times for Wales now and he's caused us no end of damage, averaging something like 17 points a match. He must really look forward to playing us!

He's scored some great tries against us, in particular the two brilliant solo efforts he produced in Dunedin in the summer of 2010.

But, more than anything, it's been his kicking game that has destroyed us – not just his kicking at goal, but where he puts us on the park.

As an openside flanker, one of your main jobs is to get into the face of the opposing outside-half, cut down his time and limit his options.

But, like all great sportsmen, Carter just seems to have so much time.

There have been times in games when I've felt I'm putting a lot of pressure on him and have nearly charged him down, only to look back and see that the ball is 60 metres downfield, back in our 22. It's so frustrating!

He can put the ball on a sixpence time and again, whether it be with a raking touch-finder, a little grubber, or a perfectly judged up-and-under.

It's not just his kicking game that's so good. He's also got the ability to make a killer break or to bring other players into the game. He's not selfish or a glory hunter by any means, and he's brilliant at letting other people shine. Because he's so dangerous and teams focus their energies on him so much, he must just sometimes think: *Right, I'll bring other players into the game now and put them in space.*

He's so naturally gifted I'd go as far as to say that I think he's one of the best players who's ever put on a pair of rugby boots.

During the 2005 British Lions series in New Zealand, he excelled himself. While as a side the All Blacks were great, he was the maestro. He was voted World Player of the Year in 2005 and rightly so.

When he and Richie McCaw are in the All Blacks, it makes a huge difference to the team.

Carter had a bit of a blip a couple of years ago when he came over to Perpignan in the south of France for a high-profile short-term move and got injured almost straight away. But he's bounced back from that and just got better and better.

Although I've played against him quite a few times, I've never had a chance to speak to him much after games. When you've played a match, particularly in Wales, and you are in the after-match function, nobody can get near him, because the world and his wife are around him asking for photographs and signings. He's a rugby superstar with the looks to match. He's clearly a David Beckham kind of character in New Zealand, and it must be difficult when you attract that kind of attention wherever you go.

But he seems to handle it well. As I say, I don't really know him well, but he seems a laid-back kind of character and very down to earth.

And he's hugely professional as well – very well schooled. He's a Canterbury boy and I've played with a lot of those who have come over to Wales, players like Ben Blair and Casey Laulala, my Cardiff Blues team-mates.

It's like a conveyer belt over there. They must have a brilliant academy system and all the players they produce seem to be both very professional and very knowledgeable.

It's rather like the old Liverpool boot room, in terms of the values they instill in players. From what I can gather, they spot the boys young and then nurture them.

They place a huge importance on your values off the field. They feel what you do off the field is very important because it has a big effect on what you do on the field. People like Carter and McCaw are from the same kind of background and you can see it in their attitude and dedication to the game.

Carter is obviously hugely naturally talented, but he must practise what he does a hell of a lot as well, especially his goal-kicking.

The only thing he hasn't done yet is win a World Cup and he will be looking to put that right this year.

Chapter Five

GEORGE SMITH

When you mention Aussie George Smith, most people probably think of the dreadlocked hairdo he sported for much of his international career. But there was so much more to George than an eye-catching hair-style. In my view, he is the most underestimated player of the professional era.

I'm a huge fan of the bloke and I don't think he gets anything like the plaudits he deserves. Probably the ultimate compliment I can give him is to say that, in my eyes, he's as good a player as Richie McCaw.

That might surprise some people, because McCaw is widely viewed as the greatest openside flanker of his generation and arguably of all time.

Don't get me wrong. I think McCaw is a legend and I make that clear later in this book. It's just that I think that, in his own way, Smith is equally good. He's so versatile.

Because Australia didn't have the strength in depth of other countries, he played a fair bit at six or No 8 during his Test career and did a great job in both roles.

If McCaw is the perfect 7, then Smith is the perfect back-rower. He's at his best on the openside flank, but he's also a very effective blindside or No 8. That's what is so amazing about him.

Most players who can play all three positions are usually much bigger, 6ft 3ins or 6ft 4ins and 17st. George is 6ft and 16st. But he's just such a good rugby player and such a tough competitor that he's been able to do it.

I think he's one of the best back-rowers there's ever been and I've come to admire him hugely over the years.

His footballing ability and his know-how is second to none. He knows the game of rugby inside out and is very, very switched on.

Because he's got a low centre of gravity, he's hugely effective at the breakdown. He's very good over the ball and very proficient at slowing down the opposition ball. His passing ability is awesome and he's even got a good kicking game, which I like as a flanker. He's a real footballer.

So he just does everything. I think he's one of the most complete players I've ever played against.

As to being hard, he's right up there. Physically he's not a big man. He's not one of those perfect physical specimens that make you think *Oh, my God* when you look at them. But he makes the most of his stature.

Apparently his test results in training aren't very high, certainly compared to someone like McCaw, whose stats are always sky-high. But when it comes to game-time, George punches way above his testing. That's the sign of a great competitor and when you combine that with his natural footballing ability, you've got a real player on your hands.

If he'd played in a great South African pack or a dominant New Zealand team, I think people would rate him up there with McCaw. And I think he deserves to be in that bracket.

You've got to remember that he's been consistently excellent despite often playing behind a struggling Aussie front five.

I've watched him for years. It was on the Lions tour of Australia in 2001 that he first really grabbed my attention.

He was so young, only twenty at the time, but he proved a dominant figure in the series. The way he took control of the breakdown after the Lions lost Richard Hill to injury midway through the second Test played a huge part in the Wallabies winning 2–1.

That was my first Lions tour and it was a strange experience especially compared to the two later trips I was to go on. In New Zealand in 2005 and South Africa in 2009, the Lions were on every TV channel and on the front and back pages of all the newspapers. Everybody knew who we were and why we were there. There was a huge fuss made about our visit.

But in Australia in 2001, there was virtually no media coverage at all. For the first month we were there, nobody batted an eyelid. It took until the first or second Test for people to sit up and take notice.

That's just a reflection of where rugby stands in the pecking order Down Under. It's not the number one sport by any means.

You've got Aussie Rules, Rugby League, cricket, even maybe soccer ahead of it. It's about the fifth or sixth sport out there, so it's difficult for them to get public attention and media exposure.

Don't get me wrong, Australia is a great place to tour. I've been lucky enough to go there a few times now and there's so much out there.

Wales can be a bit of a goldfish bowl because rugby is the number one sport, so it's nice to be out there and feel a lot more relaxed. You are not under the microscope so much, on or off the field.

But it does mean that Aussie rugby union players perhaps don't receive the recognition in their own land that they deserve.

If George Smith had been born a Kiwi, a South African or even a Welshman, he'd be a legend, considering what he's achieved in the game.

After starring in that 2001 Lions series, he went on to be ever present in the Australian squad for the rest of the decade and became the youngest ever player to play 100 Test matches. He was just twenty-nine years and four days when he brought up his century, which is phenomenal.

To play so many games at such a young age says a lot about how tough he is and his durability. He ended up with 110 caps in the end and who knows how many more he could have gone on to win if he'd kept playing Test rugby.

But he decided to call it a day at the beginning of 2010. I was amazed when I heard he'd retired from international rugby last year.

Maybe he thought he'd got 100 odd caps and felt he didn't need the hassle any more. It is tough, international rugby, and it does take its toll mentally and physically. He'd played it for ten years non-stop and probably wanted a change. So he's headed for Europe. After years and years with the Brumbies, he's moved on to play for star-studded Toulon in France, which is a big boost for European rugby.

But there's no doubt he could still cut it at international level if he wanted to. He showed that last year when he played for the Barbarians on their end-of-season tour in England and Ireland.

I was fortunate enough to be chosen for that trip as well and it was awesome to play alongside him for the Baa-Baas. He came on at half-time against England so we played left and right on the flank, and I came on for the last half hour to join him against the Irish.

It was a joy to play with him and a joy to train and spend time with him. I roomed with him as well, which is always a good way of getting to know someone.

When you play against people, you don't really get to know them well. I'd shared the odd beer with him after games before, but on this trip I shared a room with him for ten days. He is really chilled. He is from Manley, the seaside town down the coast from Sydney, and he's a bit of a beach boy. I couldn't believe how laid back he was, to be honest. He seems not to have a care in the world. But he's really polite and a very interesting person to spend time with.

He's got a similar outlook to mine in some ways. A bit old school in that he enjoyed the social side of the rugby, but you could tell that come game-day he was very, very switched on and a huge competitor.

That, together with his natural skills, is what made him such a world class player.

Perhaps, because he didn't play in a great Australian pack, his talents are less acknowledged, but, in my book, he's right up there as one of the best players in the world.

Chapter Six

JUAN-MARTIN HERNANDEZ

One of the biggest developments during my playing career has been the emergence of Argentina as a major force in world rugby. And one of the shining lights during their rise up the ranks has been the outrageously talented Juan-Martin Hernandez.

My first encounter with the Pumas was back in 1998 at Stradey Park in Llanelli. It was one of my earliest appearances for Wales and it was an eye-opening experience in more ways than one.

We won in the end, thanks to two tries from my back row partner Colin Charvis, but Argentina pushed us all over the park that night. We had quite a strong pack out, so what happened to us in the scrum was a real wake-up call and it gave us our first insight into just how strong the Pumas are as a side.

That was the beginning of their development into a genuine force and a lot of their players went on to become household names over the next few years, people like Agustin Pichot and Felipe Contepomi.

They did a good job at half-back in that game at Stradey, but it was the front row of Mauricio Reggiardo, Federico Mendez and Omar Hasan who really did the damage that night.

Since then, Argentina have gone on to produce a succession of great front rowers, bulls of men like Rodrigo Roncero and Mario Ledesma.

As a nation, they pride themselves on their scrummaging and they say their front row players are as famous as our Welsh No 10s. They are the people who get all the attention out there.

They've also produced some great back-five forwards over the past fifteen years, guys like Patricio Albacete and the Lobbe brothers.

One thing you are always guaranteed from Argentina is an outstanding pack of forwards. You know you are going to get great scrummaging from them and great loose forwards, and they are as physical as anybody you will play against.

Traditionally, they've tended to play to those strengths and have adopted very much a 10-man game.

But at the 2007 World Cup, they took their game to another level and the reason for that was Hernandez.

Prior to that tournament, he'd been best known as a free-running full-back with the Parisian club Stade Francais. But for the World Cup, the Pumas decided to hand him the reins at outside-half and it proved an inspired decision.

He was phenomenal in that tournament. His tactical kicking was outstanding, as he put the ball on a sixpence time and again. He tormented the host nation France in the opening game with a series of superb up-and-unders and never looked back.

Kicking has become a big part of the game over the last few years and sometimes it can be negative. There has been a tendency for people to overkick and there was a period when it was making the game a poor spectacle.

But if it's done well it can be hugely effective. The most successful sides over the last five years have been the ones that have kicked the most, but not just aimless kicking and booting the leather off the ball. With the best teams, it's done for the right reasons in the right areas. If you've got someone who does it properly like Hernandez, it's a very potent weapon.

With most good kickers, the rest of their game is a bit lacking. But Hernandez is a great runner and a very good defender as well, as you would expect having played a lot of his rugby at full-back.

He doesn't look as if he's very quick, but he's deceptive and very strong, and also one of the most skilful players you'll ever see. He's not lacking confidence either, as you can tell from his willingness to have a crack at a drop goal from just about anywhere.

All told, it means he's a huge threat.

And, of course, he is equally at home at either 10 or 15, which shows you just what a talented footballer he is.

Because he's not based in the UK and because he's not an All Black, a South African or a Wallaby, perhaps he doesn't get the credit he deserves.

He's been playing in France, so we don't see much of him, and we only see Argentina over here on tour once every couple of years.

So you don't see him as much as your Carters or Giteaus, but he is up there with those guys.

On his day, he's as good as anything there is. His technical ability is superb and nothing is manufactured. It's all natural. Everything seems to come easy to him. He's a bit like Gavin Henson in that he sometimes looks as if he's not bothered. But a lot of the top players look like that. They have so much time and space compared to everybody else that it's literally a walk in the park for them.

Having him at 10 gave Argentina a huge boost to their game during the last World Cup. Without him they would never have got as far as they did. They would have been a tough team to face, but he took them to a higher level. A strong pack only gets you so far. With Hernandez and Contepomi in midfield, they had that flair to back up the forward power that everyone recognises as Argentina's traditional strength.

The Pumas finished third, beating France again in the play-off and Hernandez ended up as one of the players of the tournament

Their performance in that World Cup was amazing when you think how under-resourced they are compared to the other sides. In fact they've over-achieved for some time now. They haven't got a professional league back home, which means their players are spread all over Europe, and they haven't had the luxury of organised training camps like other top nations have. They are just chucked together.

But maybe that underdog attitude it produces actually helps them. I remember watching them during their anthem before the opening World Cup game against France and I've never seen a side so pumped up in my life.

Virtually all were crying. They are an emotional nation and very passionate, and that World Cup was a rare chance for them to perform on a global platform and they were determined to make the most of it, which of course they did.

Up until now, outside of the World Cup, they've had to try and make do as best they can and satisfy themselves with the occasional game against the top teams.

But all of that is going to change next year when they join the All Blacks, the Springboks and the Wallabies to form the Four Nations tournament, which will be a tremendous boost for rugby in their country.

Let's not kid ourselves, it's going to be tough for them. If you look at New Zealand, South Africa and Australia, all their players are based at home. Very few Argentinian players actually play in Argentina, so the logistics are going to be difficult and it will be interesting to see how that pans out.

Hopefully a new batch of players will come through to meet the challenge. Pichot has already retired, while the likes of Contepomi, Ledesma and Roncero are coming towards the end of their careers.

Where they are lacking at the moment is strength in depth. They probably haven't got as many players as the other top-flight nations.

But hopefully, with the carrot of the Four Nations, a new generation will come through.

They might struggle for the first couple of years. The difficulty for them is that geographically they are so isolated.

Personally, I think it would have been great if they had joined the Six Nations. Their players are all based in France or England, so that might have made more sense.

They could have been based in Spain and played their games there. It would certainly have made for some good trips for the fans!

But, fingers crossed, it will go well for them in the Four Nations. It will add some variety to the existing Tri Nations, and Argentina definitely need to be nurtured for the good of the world game.

It's no good them just competing once every four years in the World Cup. They need stepping stones along the way. At the moment they have one-off internationals in the summer and autumn, but there's nothing like a tournament-based structure for development of the game, which is what they need.

Hopefully, with Hernandez leading the way, they can go on to make a real impact in the Four Nations tournament and solidify their status as a real force in the world game.

Chapter Seven

GETHIN JENKINS

The first time I met Gethin Jenkins wasn't on the rugby field or on a training pitch.

It was back in the 1999–2000 season and he was just starting out with my home-town club of Pontypridd. But I had left Ponty by then to join Cardiff, so I didn't know him. However, in the Welsh squad at the time was Geraint Lewis, the Ponty back rower, who was from the same neck of the woods as Gethin, in the Llantwit Fardre/Beddau area, and I remember after one training session, Geraint saying: "Melonhead is working in McDonald's tonight, let's go and see him because he sorts the boys out with extra chips."

For a start, that shows how unprofessional we were back then. But it was also the first time I'd ever heard of the "Melon", the name Gethin is known by throughout the game, because of the shape of his head! And the most memorable thing about him from back then was that he used to work in McDonald's!

(I really wanted to put that story in here, because I know he'll hate it!)

Since that first meeting, I've gone on to spend a hell of a lot of time in Melon's company – probably too much, if truth be told.

He's been my training partner for years and he's one of my closest friends in the game.

So if anyone's qualified to give the low-down on the real Gethin Jenkins I guess it's me.

I've said before that he could moan for Wales and that's certainly true. If there was a Welsh moaning side, he'd be the captain!

Whether it's the food, the weather, the training or whatever, he'll find something wrong with it. I suppose I can moan a bit as well, but he's got it down to an art.

After a while, you just get used to it and take it with a pinch of salt. When you know him well, it's quite funny.

He still moans, but in a slightly different way now that he's taken on a leadership role as a senior player with the Cardiff Blues and Wales. He takes that role very seriously and he's harsh on other players if they are not pulling their weight in training. If they are doing something wrong, he'll tell them in no uncertain terms.

I think that frankness is something we lack in Wales. At the top end of the game, that's what you've got to do. Gethin doesn't do it just for the sake of it, but because he knows if that player makes the same mistake on the Saturday it will cost everybody.

He is also such an intelligent rugby player, which he doesn't always get credit for. He loves the game and knows it inside out. How many loose-head props do you know who would give a debrief on a defensive session? But that's the kind of thing he does. He's got an opinion on everything in the game and he isn't afraid to share it with you.

Ben Blair, the Cardiff Blues full-back, says Geth is the only prop in the world who will tell the outside-half how to run the game! He'll tell them when they should kick, when they should run, when it's on. It's just the way he is.

We hit it off straight away once he joined the Welsh squad in 2002. He came through from Ponty with the likes of Michael Owen, Robert Sidoli, Mefin Davies and Ceri Sweeney, when Wales's Kiwi coach Steve Hansen shipped out the old boys and brought the new faces in.

That's when I got to know Geth properly and we clicked from the start. The following year he joined Cardiff and I've known him really well since then.

We are from very similar backgrounds and have quite similar outlooks. We both train hard and we've always done extra sessions together.

I think we are both very stubborn and competitive. One thing you are taught when you are from our part of the world is you don't get anything easy, you have to earn it.

At times during my career, people have told me I'm too small and I've always had a battle to prove people wrong. But I've thrived on it. That's how I am, and Gethin's the same. We are both really competitive and want to be the best we can be. We've never sat back on our laurels. We've both always wanted to perform at the highest level we can.

We are pretty down-to-earth and grounded as well. We've both still got our old mates from Ponty from way back when. There's always good banter between us and it's been good for me to know him. I'm a few years older and it's been great to see him come through as this youngster from Pontypridd and develop into one of the best props in the world.

At the start of his international career, he was tried out as tight-head and some people said he couldn't scrummage. But he's gone on to prove his doubters wrong in emphatic fashion.

I know he can do a coach's head in at times. He's got a very dry sense of humour and he can break a coach! He's never happy with anything a coach does. Either a training session is too long, too short, too easy or too hard.

But once coaches get to know him, they appreciate him for what he is. At Steve Hansen's leaving do in 2004 he said that if there was one player he could take back with him to New Zealand, it would be Gethin.

For a Kiwi to say that shows how good Gethin really is. But Hansen knew what he had in Geth.

Initially when coaches start coaching him, they think *Oh my God*. But, later, they all want him in their side.

I know I'm biased because he's a mate, but I think he's the best loose-head in the world. He's revolutionised the position. Every up-and-coming loose-head is compared to Geth these days.

His stats are phenomenal, in terms of his work-rate and the amount of tackles he makes. A lot of props put themselves in positions where they don't have to make a tackle. But Geth leads the way in defence. He's got a freakish engine for a man of his size and great skills. He's a good footballer and loves to get the ball in his hands.

If truth be told, he's a frustrated back rower. There's many a time where he tells me what I should be doing. I take it with a pinch of salt now. But it is like having another back row forward when he's playing. It makes it so much easier for you when he's in the defensive line with you.

I joke with him sometimes that if they banned scrums he'd be happy, but I actually think he's hugely underrated in that part of his game. He's a really good scrummager.

And while he does enjoy carrying the ball, he's just as happy smashing rucks and making tackles.

He's the whole package as far as I'm concerned. Definitely the best prop I've played with.

The fact that he's been the Test loose-head on two Lions tours speaks for itself really.

On the last trip to South Africa in 2009, he was faced with a challenge for the Test spot from England's Andrew Sheridan.

There was a big push by the English press to get Sheri in there and Sheri is a great player, but Geth was one of first names on the team-sheet. I think he enjoyed that challenge and he relished the whole experience.

Given that Warren Gatland, Shaun Edwards and Rob Howley were all on the coaching team, the way we played for the Lions was obviously much the way we played for Wales.

Speaking to the tour skipper Paul O'Connell, I found out that Geth was explaining the patterns to the Irish boys, which they found a bit unusual coming from a prop!

But that's him. He's a very intelligent rugby player and he's not backward in coming forward when it comes to giving an opinion on the game or speaking his mind.

I think he has probably mellowed a little bit over the years, but he still keeps everyone on their toes. No one ever sits back when he's about.

And there are little things that tickle me about Geth.

He is sociable, but if he doesn't have to speak to anybody after training I think he's quite happy for the rest of the day!

He loves his Facebook and his video games

like *Call of Duty*. He is quite happy to shut himself away in his room with his games or go on Facebook. All he does apart from that is sleep and train!

And I know he has this image of being a bit grumpy and hard work at times, but he's a very generous bloke and a little softie deep down.

And he'll hate me saying that too!

Chapter Eight

MATT GITEAU

Everyone knows that the Aussies are sports-mad and ultracompetitive. It's ingrained in them.

But, in my view, when it comes to rugby, they are also the most inventive nation in the world.

They are always the first to think up new things and try out new ideas. They've got great coaches out there and they are always ready to think outside the box.

I think it's in their nature. They are full of self-belief and have the confidence to try different things.

There's also the fact that the Wallabies have never really had a dominant tight five in recent times, so they've become hugely inventive in their back play, looking to make the absolute most of whatever set-piece ball they do win.

And they've also looked to develop a fluid, fast-moving game, where everybody from 1 to 15 is comfortable with the ball in hand. Whether you are a prop, a hooker or a second row, you are expected to be able to pass the ball. It's not just head down, backside up for the forwards.

Having been coached by Scott Johnson – the former Wales skills guru – I know that is very much the Aussie way. He didn't care what number you had on your back. To him, you were first a rugby player and you were expected to be able to give and take a pass whether you were a prop or an outside-half.

And if one current player sums up that country's inventive approach to the game it's Matt Giteau.

He's someone who is always looking to try something different out on the pitch and who has the confidence and self-belief to keep on trying new things even when they don't always work.

The way the Wallabies have used Giteau over the years reflects their innovative approach to the game. Plenty of players have lined up at both 10 and 12, with the positions becoming pretty interchangeable in recent times. And one or two have switched between scrum-half and fly-half, with the French duo of Freddie Michalak and Jean-Baptiste Ellisalde being good examples.

But nobody I can think of has played at 9, 10 and 12 in Test rugby – nobody, that is, apart from Matt Giteau.

For him to be able to play in all three positions at the highest level of the game shows how talented a rugby player he is.

It was on the 2006 autumn tour of Europe that the Aussies decided to select him at scrum-half. It was Scott Johnson's brainwave – he had by then moved on from Wales to coach in his homeland.

I think Scott's idea was that Giteau was their best player, so he wanted to get the ball in his hands as often as possible – and that meant playing him at nine.

It was a bold move because Giteau hadn't played there since he was at school. Ahead of the game against Wales at the Millennium Stadium there was a lot of talk about it being a gamble that could backfire badly.

You could understand this, as scrum-half is such a unique, specialist position. That's why you take three of them to a World Cup. It's not something a player can just slip into.

But then Giteau is no ordinary player.

As it turned out, he was close on Man of the Match and scored a memorable individual try – he caught us all napping by taking a quick tap penalty and darting over.

He played really well that day and didn't

look out of place at all. That shows he's absolute class.

Because he's so good it's been a case of trying to find his best position, and there's been a lot of debate on this through his career.

I first remember watching Giteau when he was coming through at the Brumbies in the old Super 12 competition Down Under and you could tell he was something special then.

Over the years, he's switched back and forth between outside-half and inside centre, creating havoc in both positions.

He's not one of those manufactured 10s who runs the game in a programmed way. He's very, very instinctive. That can be a good or a bad thing in your side, but it's definitely hard when you play against him. You just never know what he's going to do and you've got to be on your toes the whole time.

He sees things that other players don't and he's got the confidence to try things. He's not afraid to make a mistake, either.

Sometimes that gets him into trouble and he maybe doesn't run a game how some people want him to. But he's one of those players spectators will pay to see over and over again because he's willing to do something different every time.

He's obviously a big star in Australia and he got a huge contract to go over to Perth a few years ago and join the new Western Force team. Now he's back at the Brumbies and as big a star as ever.

But, when you meet him, he's down-to-earth and a really good bloke.

He's just one of the boys off the field and a real character, as I discovered when we linked up to play for the Barbarians against South Africa in November 2007.

On that Baa-Baas trip, he and Justin Marshall, the Kiwi scrum-half, more or less ran the week, both on and off the field, from a social and rugby point of view. You need those sort of characters on a trip like that.

Playing for the Barbarians is a real treat for me as it's like stepping back to the early days of my career when rugby was more of a social sport. Some people definitely thrive better in that Baa-Baas environment than others, and personally I love it, and I think the same went for Matt, who showed what a class act he is both on and off the field.

Training with the Baa-Baas is perhaps not very structured, but you do play a lot of touch rugby and his skills in that were incredible.

The great thing when you play for the

Barbarians is you really enjoy yourself throughout the week.

You haven't prepared anything like you would for an international, but come the match, the top boys put their game heads on. Giteau definitely fell into that category. Come game-day he was really competitive.

When you play in those matches, it's brilliant to see players freed of the shackles they usually wear.

The game now is so results-orientated and there's so much pressure to win at all costs, that some teams are perhaps over-coached. So it's great to go out and just try things. You can be yourself. As you can imagine, Giteau revelled in that opportunity and he was awesome in that game against the Springboks.

Some of the breaks he made were amazing and the way he put other players, like Ma'a Nonu, into space was pure class. Playing off him was so easy, which was remarkable considering we'd never played together before. That shows what a good player he is and what a team player he is as well.

I'd watched him play a lot on TV over the years and also lined up against him a few times. But it's only when I actually played with him that I realised just how good he is.

He's very vocal during the game, organising the forwards and backs and calling the moves.

He's really sharp and so aware of people around him. He's one of the best support runners I've ever seen. He's scored a hell of a lot of tries and that's because he's so sharp and runs great support lines, so that when somebody makes a break he's almost always there on their shoulder.

He's also defensively strong, as you would expect from the son of a former rugby league player. He's only a little guy, but he's as tough as nails as well.

He's run the show for the Aussies for most of his career, so perhaps it hasn't helped him that he's had to do the goal-kicking. That's a lot to take on and he's had one or two off-days with the boot over the years.

But he's always been prepared to carry on taking the shots at goal, which shows his character and self-belief as there's huge pressure involved in being a place-kicker in Test rugby.

That's Matt Giteau for you, a typical Aussie both on and off the field.

Chapter Nine

BRIAN O'DRISCOLL

Whenever anyone asks me what makes Irishman Brian O'Driscoll such a special player, I always give the same answer: "Tell me something he can't do."

To my mind, Dricco is not far off the perfect rugby player.

He's got a great set of wheels, he can offload, he can throw a 20-metre pass off both hands, he's got great footwork and he's a very good kicker of the ball, whether it's a long kick, a grubber or a chip.

Defensively he's as hard as nails, always making his tackles, and he's an absolute pest at the breakdown, as good as any 7 you've ever played against.

Really, he's like three or four players rolled into one. He's quick enough to be a winger, he's like an extra back rower with the way he contests at the tackle area, and he can kick the ball better than a lot of fly-halves.

And, of course, he's not a bad centre either. He's got all the attacking and defensive strengths you need to play in that position.

As a complete rugby player, there are very few to match him. Like I say, tell me a weakness he's got?

The first time I really sat up and took notice of him was when he scored a hat-trick of tries for Ireland against France out in Paris in 2000. I remember thinking to myself *God, who's this*?

Then, the following year, I got to see him close up when we were both selected for the 2001 Lions tour of Australia.

He really came into his own on that trip. I was in awe of him.

He was still so young back then, just twenty-two, but he ran riot, especially in the first Test against the Wallabies in Brisbane.

I was on the bench that night and it was a joy to watch him. He was unstoppable. It was as good an individual performance as I've seen.

He's always been rapid, but he was so quick in those days and the Aussies couldn't cope with him. He had the gas to go outside people and the strength to break tackles at will.

He set one try up for the Welsh winger Dafydd James in the first half and then scored a superb individual try himself after the break when he tore the home defence apart.

He was just amazing in that first Test and a key factor in our convincing win.

I remember hearing the Lions fans singing "Waltzing O'Driscoll" to the tune of "Waltzing Matilda" as they left the ground. It was Dricco's night and it was a performance that established him as a true world star.

Then, four years later, he was back as a Lion again, and this time as skipper for the 2005 tour of New Zealand under Clive Woodward.

I know he saw it as a huge honour to lead the Lions and he was desperate for us to be successful.

So what happened to him out there must have been very difficult to deal with.

Within 90 seconds of the opening Test against the All Blacks in Christchurch, his tour was over, when he suffered a serious shoulder injury.

A lot was made of it at the time, with suggestions that he had been speared, but for Brian himself it was just really bad luck and painful in more ways than one.

As Lions captain, the last thing you want to do is go home early but he had to go back for a shoulder operation. And although Gareth

Thomas stepped up and did a great job as skipper, Brian's absence definitely had a big effect on that tour.

He's such a good player and such a talisman. Certain players have that presence.

Just knowing that Brian O'Driscoll is in your side makes a hell of a difference.

Ireland have found it as well. When he's not in the side, they aren't quite the same.

Having suffered such an unhappy ending to that 2005 tour, Dricco must have been determined to make a big impact when he was selected for his third Lions trip last year – and he certainly did that.

Some critics had started to question whether he was quite as good as he had been, but he provided the perfect answer during 2009.

First, he captained Ireland to their first Grand Slam since 1948, then he won the Heineken Cup with Leinster, and then had a great Lions tour of South Africa to show he was as good as ever.

What summed him up on that trip was the huge hit he made on Danie Roussouw, the Springboks forward in the second Test in Pretoria. He put absolutely everything into it, against a guy twice his size, and cleaned him out. Dricco didn't know where he was afterwards but he still carried on, as he's done so often during his career.

Time and again in matches, we've seen him get up and continue playing when it seemed certain there was no way he could go on. That's the kind of competitor he is.

It's no coincidence that my Cardiff and Wales team-mate Jamie Roberts improved so much playing alongside Brian in the centre on last year's Lions tour. Jamie played awesomely and deserved to be named player of the series, but he will say himself that Brian played a huge part in that.

They are two very different types of players and complemented each other very well.

I've been fortunate enough to go on three Lions tours with Brian now and I've got on really well with him.

He's a down-to-earth guy and good value off the field. He likes the social side of tours and like the majority of the Irish players, he's very good fun.

He's a superstar in Ireland with a very high profile. Rugby has skyrocketed in popularity over there in the last five to ten years and he's found himself at the centre of that.

But he's still remained very level-headed

and grounded. He never goes out looking for attention.

When I've been with him on tour, he's just happy with the boys having a few quiet beers. I think it's difficult for him to do that in Ireland. Maybe he enjoys it on tour because he can relax more when he gets away.

But he's also a very proud Irishman and a great ambassador for his country.

He's also very good as a public speaker, good with the media and, as a captain, good in the way he talks to referees. Brian is very intelligent and says the right things at the right times, whatever the situation.

He's also typically Irish in that he's got the self-belief that sometimes we lack in Wales.

I've played with and against some great centres in my career, people like Tana Umaga, Yannick Jauzion, Will Greenwood, Pieter Muller and Tom Shanklin.

Greenwood was absolute class, a very intelligent rugby player, while Pieter is the best defensive centre I've ever seen. He was a beast of a man and great to play alongside during his time at Cardiff. As for Tom, he's always played well against O'Driscoll. That's a badge of honour for any centre. Over the years, the bigger the game the better Tom has played.

So there have been some great centres around in my time, but for me Brian is at the top of the tree.

His natural talent has obviously played a big part in that, but there's more to it.

Some players you look at and think what perfect specimens they are physically. Brian's not like that. He's not a huge man. But he's got that natural rugby strength and every time he runs and goes into contact he puts everything into it, every single sinew.

He's not as big as the likes of Jauzion or Umaga, but he matches them in terms of impact. He's somebody who really runs his weight and you know when Dricco runs at you.

He's as tough as old boots and if any captain leads by example, he does. He's someone everyone in the game has a huge amount of respect for, on and off the field.

I would go as far as to say he's the best British or Irish player of my generation.

The others from these isles that I have chosen in my top ten – Martin Johnson, Shane Williams and Gethin Jenkins – have all got their strengths and they are all good at certain things.

But Dricco is the complete player and that's what makes him the best.

Chapter Ten

RICHIE McCAW

He's been called a cheat, he's been called a freak, but to me he's simply the greatest number 7 there's ever been.

As someone who has spent his career playing in the position, I obviously pay particular attention to other people who occupy the openside flank.

And in my opinion, New Zealand's Richie McCaw is in a league of his own.

It's because he's so good that people have tried to cast doubt over what he does by calling him a cheat.

Team after team have brought up the C-word over the years, maybe to try and influence referees, or get under McCaw's skin.

But it doesn't work. It's like water off a duck's back to him.

It's the ultimate compliment for a 7 to be called a cheat. If somebody called me one I'd definitely be flattered.

It was funny last year when I was presented with the ERC Fair Play award, to coincide with fifteen years of Heineken Cup rugby. It was a real honour, but I was also a little bit disappointed. As my skipper at the Cardiff Blues, Paul Tito, said at the time, you can't be doing your job properly as a 7 if you are picking up a fair play award!

As an openside, you are paid to push the laws to their limit and McCaw does that better than anyone. You certainly won't hear me complaining that he's cheating. He just does his job, superbly well.

There are so many times he could have been yellow carded but hasn't. I think sometimes you make your own luck and he's learned over the years how to do that.

You ask any player and he's just what you want in your side – an absolute pain in the backside to the opposition.

What he does isn't cheating in my book. It's not cynical, like handball to score a goal in football – like Maradona's "Hand of God" against England in the 1986 World Cup.

What he does is push the laws to the edge, and get away with what he can. That's top level sport.

McCaw knows the breakdown is one such grey area, so he pushes it as far as he can. I bet he's penalised as much as anybody else, but for every time he gets penalised, he gets away with it two or three times more.

He studies referees. That's the modern game. You always have your referee reports and everybody knows what certain refs will let you get away with. As someone who has played 7, I know that's the case.

I've met Richie a couple of times and know he's very intelligent. He's very shrewd in the way he handles conflict. He's captain of New Zealand and a very good one, but he also knows that this helps him get away with a bit more.

It's a big call for a referee to send a captain off. There have been a few times where if he had been just a 7 he might have gone, but because he's skipper he's got away with it.

He's also in the referee's ear a lot and is very careful how he speaks to them.

But there's far more to his game than pushing the laws and being cute with refs. For me, he's the perfect 7.

I remember, years ago, Steve Hansen coming over from Canterbury to coach Wales and telling me, "We've got this kid coming through."

McCaw had only just started playing for the All Blacks then and nobody knew him. But I remember Hansen telling me he was going to be something special and, of course, he was right.

The fact that he's the only person to have been named IRB World Player of the Year twice speaks for itself.

He's just streets ahead of everyone else in his position and one of the main reasons why New Zealand are so good.

When people call him a freak, they are spot on. He is a freak, but in the nicest possible way.

He's crazily athletic. All his test results are sky-high and he backs them up out on the pitch. I don't know if there's ever been a more consistent player in the game.

It's hard, if not impossible, to remember a bad McCaw performance. An average game for him would be a high-quality one for 99 per cent of players.

I've obviously studied him more than most people as he's a fellow 7 and what he does never ceases to amaze me. Generally, success as an openside is reliant on others. Your game depends very much on how your team is doing. If they're going well and are you are on the front foot it's a joy to play at 7 and a lot easier to make an impact.

If you are on the back foot, it's a very different story. When your pack isn't going well, your set-piece is struggling and your backline is being cut to shreds, it can be a long day at the office.

But with McCaw, it doesn't seem to matter what's going on around him. He still seems to have a huge influence on proceedings.

When I watch Super 14 or Tri Nations games involving him, I start meaning to watch the match in general, but I invariably end up watching what he's doing rather than watching the whole game, because he is so remarkable.

I remember watching him in one Tri Nations match against the Springboks in South Africa and he simply dominated the game. As a 7 it's very hard to do that. It's easier if you are a 10, but he single-handedly won the game that day.

If there any budding opensides out there, my advice to them would be to put on a tape of Richie McCaw, and watch!

As a 7, you've got the job of trying to be involved in everything, in both attack and defence. You've got to try and be a pain in the backside for the opposition and spoil their ball as much as you can. Then, in attack, you want to try and get the ball in your hands and support as much as you can.

McCaw does both better than anyone. He's always on the move. He's making tackles, he's hitting rucks, he's up on his feet so quick and involved in so many breakdowns.

Sometimes when you are playing against him, you see him pop up at a ruck and you think: *How has he got there? He shouldn't be there, he was at another ruck on the other side of field a few seconds ago!* But somehow he does it, time and again.

To be able to do what he does, you have to be ridiculously fit and he clearly puts in a huge amount of work in training and really looks after himself.

He's not hugely muscular. If you look at David Pocock, the young Australian openside who is going to be one of the best, he's built like a body-builder. Richie's not like that. He's not a big guy, not muscle-bound.

But he's very wiry, with real natural raw strength and he's also an amazing competitor who uses every ounce of power to good effect.

You can see that particularly with his ball-carrying. He loves to get the ball in his hands and consistently makes good ground, making the most of his natural strength.

On top of all that, he reads the game superbly.

With McCaw, you've got fitness and intelligence combined. He's always in the right place at the right time and just makes the right decisions. He's got that Kiwi trait of thinking differently to other players. He's the classic streetwise New Zealander. I think that comes because they just live and breathe the game. They are so rugby-intelligent and so switched on.

I would say that McCaw and another All Black, Michael Jones, are the best 7s there have ever been.

I was just starting to get into rugby when Jones was playing in the late 1980s and early 1990s and his athleticism revolutionised openside play at the time.

McCaw has done the same now and brought a whole new dimension to the contact area, which has become more important than ever in the game. When he's about, he's made it the place the game is won and lost.

I've spoken to him a few times after games, when I've sat next to him at dinners, and he's a very unassuming, classy individual.

It's hard to get an All Blacks jersey, but I've been fortunate enough that he's swapped with me a couple of times. For someone who is a superstar, he's a very easy guy to speak to.

As well as being a great rugby player, he's also a qualified pilot. He's just good at everything he does and a top bloke as well.

I wouldn't put myself in his bracket as an openside. He's in a different league to me. But it's an honour to have been a rival of his on the international stage.

To my mind, he's the greatest there's ever been – the perfect 7.

Quick Reads

Books in the Quick Reads series

Quick Reads 📖

Great stories, great writers, great entertainment

Trouble on the Heath
Terry Jones

Accent Press

A comedy of Russian gangsters, town planners and a dog called Nigel.

Malcolm Thomas is not happy. The view he loves is about to be blocked by an ugly building. He decides to take action and forms a protest group. Then things go badly wrong and Malcolm finds himself running for his life. Along the way he gets mixed up with corrupt town planners, violent gangsters, and a kidnapped concert pianist. Malcolm starts to wonder if objecting to the building was such a good idea when he finds himself upside down with a gun in his mouth.

This hilarious story from Monty Python star, Terry Jones, will make you laugh out loud.

Quick Reads

Great stories, great writers, great entertainment

Worlds Beyond Words
Alison Stokes

Accent Press

A collection of real-life stories from people who have improved their lives through better literacy.

Some people take the power of words for granted. But for the thousands of people who struggle with poor literacy, words can be scary things.

The men and women featured in this book have overcome their fears to improve their reading later in life.

Whether they are famous businessmen or sports stars, teenagers in care, middle-aged mums, young soldiers or refugees forced to flee bloodshed in their own home countries, they all share a common desire to learn. Their stories will inspire others to follow journeys of their own.

Quick Reads

Great stories, great writers, great entertainment

The Flying Pineapple
Jamie Baulch

Accent Press

With his blond dreadlocks and his speed on the running track, Jamie Baulch earned the nickname 'The Flying Pineapple'.

This is Jamie's story about his life as one of the most successful athletes in Britain.

His life on the track was always about how fast he could run – as he won medals at the Olympics and World Championships.

He puts his success down to his adoptive parents who inspired him to be the best he could be.

Since his retirement in 2005, he has not slowed down and now as head of a sports management company continues to inspire a new generation of sportsmen and women.

He was awarded a World Championship gold medal as part of the British relay team 13 years after the event, when the original American winners were disqualified for using drugs.

Quick Reads 📖

Great stories, great writers, great entertainment

The Hardest Test
Scott Quinnell

Accent Press

Scott Quinnell is one of the best-known names in rugby. He played both rugby league and rugby union, for Wales and for the British Lions. He was captain of the Welsh team seven times and won 52 caps.

But amidst all this success, Scott had a painful secret. He struggled to read. In *The Hardest Test*, he describes his struggle against learning difficulties throughout his childhood and his journey towards becoming one of the best rugby players in Britain. When he retired from rugby in 2005 he continued his battle with dyslexia in order to change both his and his children's lives.

Quick Reads

Great stories, great writers, great entertainment

Life's New Hurdles
Colin Jackson

Accent Press

Colin Jackson is one of the greatest athletes that Britain has ever produced. He was in the world top ten for 16 years, and was world number 1 for two of them. He set seven European and Commonwealth and nine UK records, and he still holds the world record for indoor hurdling.

In 2003 Colin retired from athletics in front of an adoring home crowd. Then real life began. In Life's New Hurdles Colin describes the shock of adjusting to sudden change. How would he manage without the strict routine of training and competing that had been his life since the age of 17? Would he forever long to be back on the track? And how satisfying would his new career be as a sports presenter and television personality? From athletics commentating to *Strictly Come Dancing*, Colin describes the challenges and joys of starting a whole new life.

About the Author

Known as "Nugget", **Martyn Williams** is one of the most popular figures in the rugby world. He first made his name as a young flanker for his home-town club Pontypridd in the mid-1990s. For the past 15 years has been a major player in the Welsh squad. He has featured in two Grand Slam-winning campaigns and was named Player of the Six Nations in 2005. He has captained his country on many occasions and has been on three British Lions tours, to Australia, New Zealand and South Africa. After leaving Pontypridd in 1999, he joined Cardiff Blues and has been with the club ever since. In 2010 he was granted a testimonial.

Quick Reads 📖

Great stories, great writers, great entertainment

Team Calzaghe
Michael Pearlman

Accent Press

Never beaten in 46 fights, Joe Calzaghe became recognised as one of the greatest sportsmen in British history after his last fight against American great Roy Jones at New York's Madison Square Garden.

The man behind his success is father and trainer Enzo Calzaghe, who has produced four world champions from his tiny South Wales gym.

Team Calzaghe is a fascinating book which explores the success of the Calzaghe boxing family, which includes Enzo Maccarinelli, Bradley Pryce, Gary Lockett and Gavin Rees.

It also lifts the lid on the boxers' battles with booze, bulimia and the authorities as the Calzaghes defied their critics to rule the boxing world.